unNatural Heart

by

Geoff Francis

Published in Great Britain in 2020 by Bonobo TV

This edition 2020

Copyright © 2020 Bonobo TV

Words and original photographs by Geoff Francis

ISBN 978-1-907729-19-5

Edited by Jacky Francis Walker

Designed by Paul Windridge

www.bonobo.tv

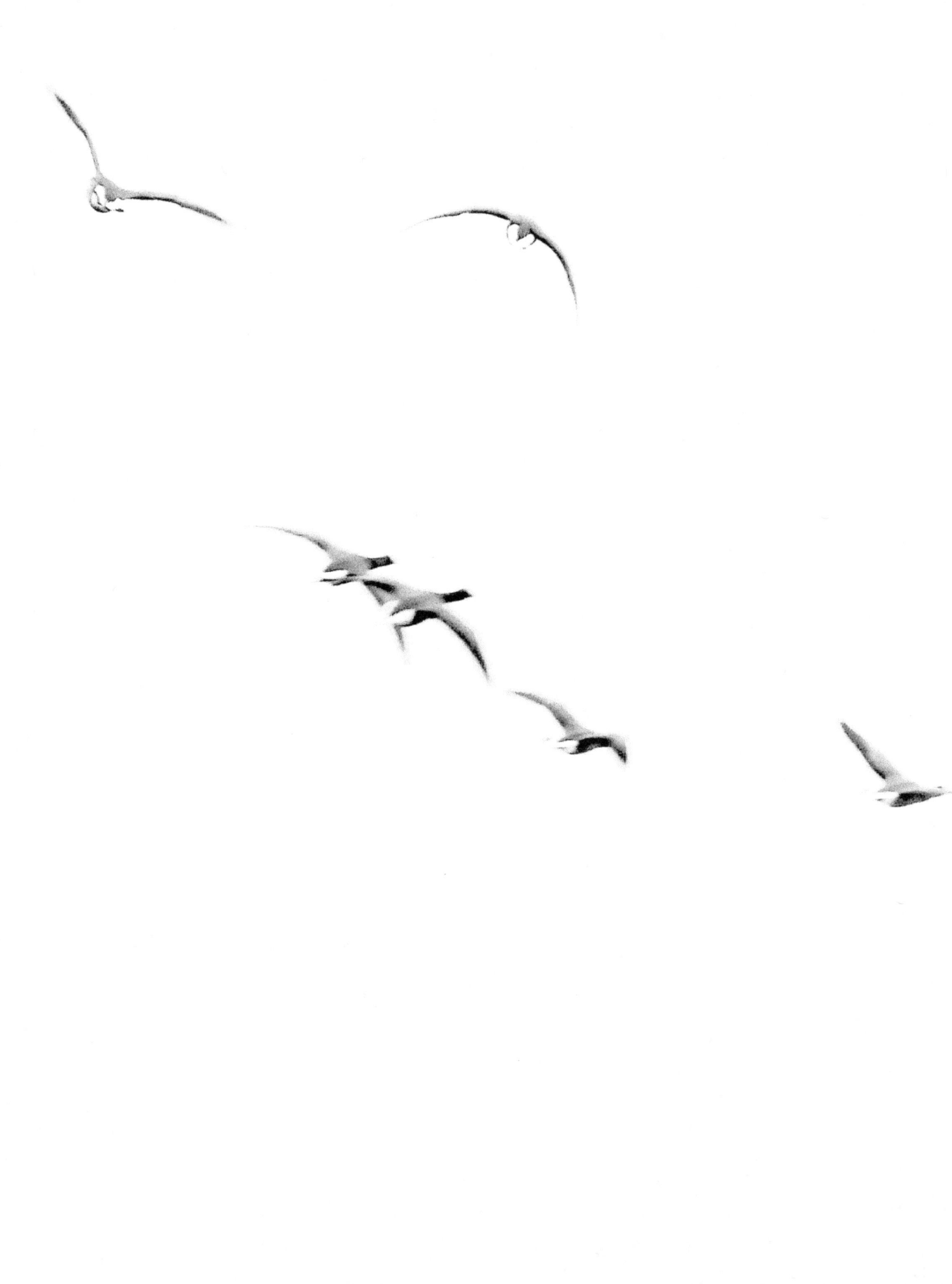

unNatural Heart

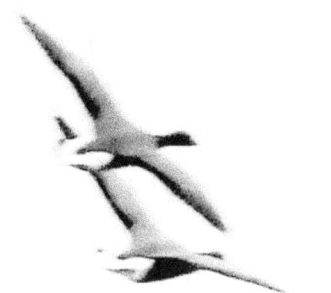

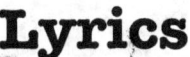

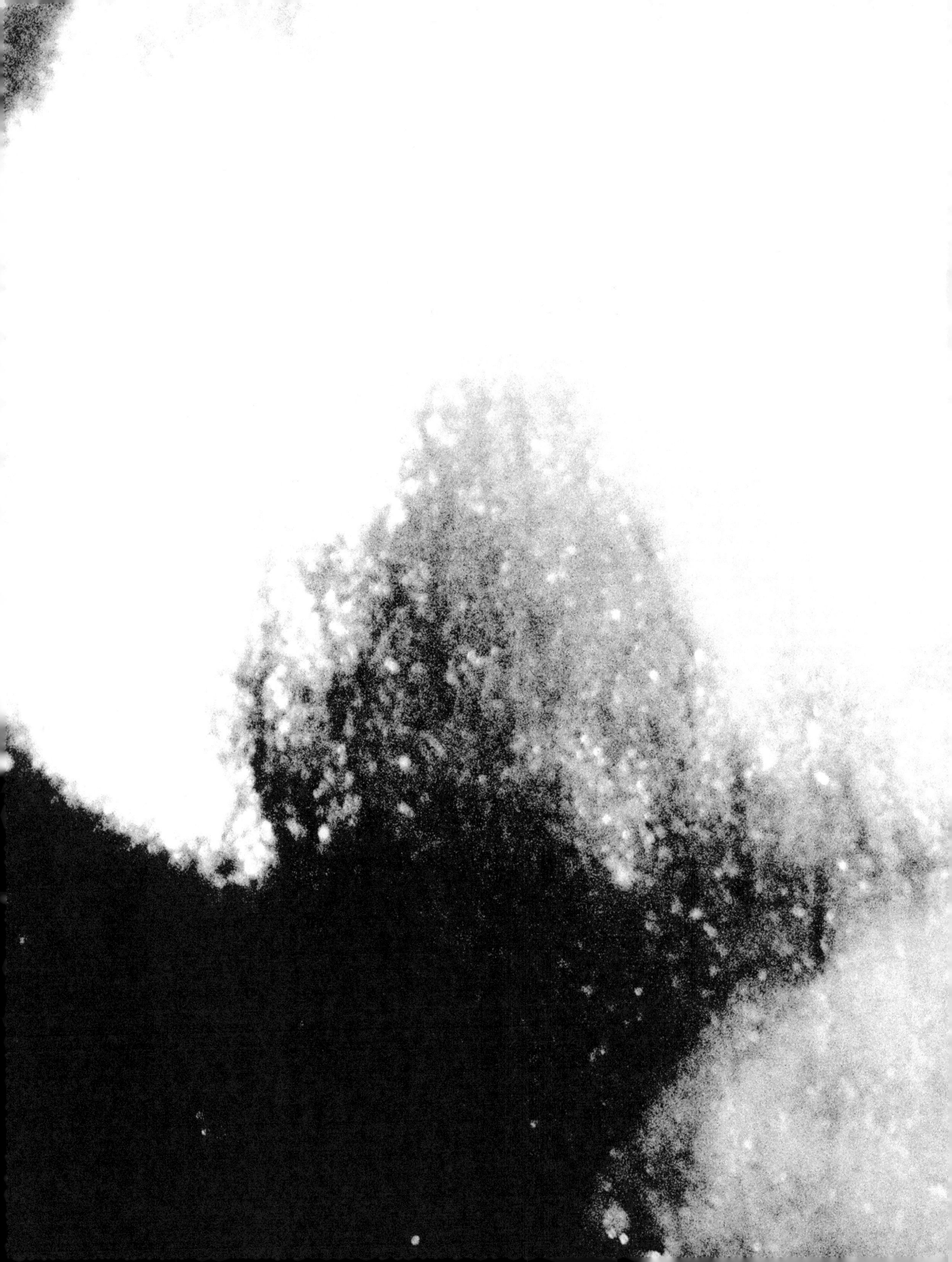

Connection

Love is the thread by which

we hold onto and are held by life

The quality of that thread determines

whether ours is an existence of delight

or misery

of indifference or celebration

Like dolphins at play

You are delight

we are celebration

Still

a dozen crows

on winter wood

stand sentry

over the stillness

hard against

the clear blue

of the day

three dogs

lead their humans

along the river path

without them

life would be a lesser place

just breath

without a meaning

for drawing it

The reeds and spring

call from within

their frozen fortress

a reprise of

randomly recalled joy

lived once

in the same life

refreshing

a hoped for future

Each moment

a delight

as he awaited

An inevitable encounter

not knowing

what it was to be

Each day

held in it

a dozen things

he would share

the joy

and enthusiasm

of a puppy

or a calf

for their newly gifted life

the bemused ostrich

as it witnessed

his morning exercise

the blackbird

calling

perched high

above the river

its reflection

untrammelled

in the barely

moving

dark water

two rare birds

spotted

in an unrare place

a swan cob

fervently gathering

common straw

as his pen

surveys

from the top

of the mound

which will be

their next nest

a rude swing

hanging still

in

the unbroken peace

of a ' perfect garden '

an unseasonal brazier

firing orange

through

a rusted aperture

a breath-catching-scent

of

an unknown

unseen

flower

the unexpected energy

of a rusty dog

as she turned

her outward plodding

to the homeward path

the soft rain

which gently

troubled the water

circling the surface

into

an endless perfection

as leaves left untroubled

the early bee

but peace

formed

no coalition

with his world

Next day a dozen More

the pen now sitting
atop her eggs
content now
after her rebukes

a common
blue flower
electrifying
the shadows

a full rounded
dandelion head
awaiting a breeze
to count its hours

fragile hope filled lives
crossing the water
behind
a mallard mother

how the smallest bird
lightning cracks
the silent sky
with its giant voice

soft munching
of the Highland cattle
as night falls
across THEIR field

the strength
in the lean muscle
of the mare
that greeted him
every morning
shared his breath
with hers
to know his truth

the rejected calf
one day old
suckling
from a bottle

delicate
lost dog
thin
nervous
Beautiful
in the strength
of its fragility

Heron
soft in grey
with a deadly beak
unstinting
in its stillness

A hill to climb

Up above it all
An endless sea

A chair so high
I can kick my legs
And be a child

Again

And watch
In peace
salvaged charges
As a donkey
Bugles
His delight
Upon the evenings tranquility

After the Rain

After the rain
When nature
had softened
Leaf and branch
Their voices rang
so clear

Righteous Envy

he had always
envied animals
their sense of purpose
moved by the need
to express
What is naturally
inside them
Unencumbered by choice
they slip easily
into the rhythm of destiny

Anonymous

In the night
His spirit drifted
Softly over the earth

Making no Mark
Where it touched

observing only
As birds
Struggled
hunkered against
the dank darkness
unwilling to try
to move or fly

Anting

Wings spread wide
A black crow
anting
Close upon the earth
Content
In worshipping the sun

Until anxious humanity
Crept too close

There was a lesson here
Who was teaching whom

The answer was clear

If we choose to see
Unprejudiced
By toxic words
Of sensation seeking
Alcoholic drug driven
Journalism and its masters

Lesson

He sat on the Sundeck
Watching the amber listed gull

its terrible dread beak
Gently stripped
with the appropriate force
Every part
Of the apricot fruit
He had placed there
For the purpose

Succeeding adroitly
With skilful ease
Where he had failed

Innocent Possibilities

Two pairs of brown eyes
fixed each other
Across an empty beach

Body and tail
Signalled innocent possibilities
Of temporary games

Demanding voices
commanded obedience
which would never
let them be

Spirits in the sky

obscured

from

distant

indistinct

landfalls

shrouded in a late mist

two Seagulls

played

in the uplift

almost touched

tumbled

rose and fell

in

uncertain

unexpected

delight

delivering them

to the winds

spiriting them

holding them

separate

and close

Signal

The wind blows the tree

through the leaves

the street lamp

flashes semaphores

onto the wall

like an ancient

Buddha's mysterious clue

The Wood Pigeon

Plumped up

Subtle shades

Of mauve and Pink

Gorgeous grey

Silhouetted

And softly radiant

Against a flat grey sky

The wood pigeon

Confidently rides

A fragile branch

Above the river

Winter wonder

Sunbright sharp
a gull defeated
the frozen ground
with its flight

as the snow
melted
a male blue tit
puffed up
against the remaining cold
drew from the air
what warmth
it could
and cast its thin voice
into the skies
to tempt a mate

he opened
the window willingly
to the damp cold
of the morning
and
let in the beauty
of the birds
chorusing
their hopeful aspirations

Sun so bright
He had to cover
his eyes

A day to be lived for
a day he wished

He could plant
Compassion
In every heart

So they could see
These things

Evanescent

Baby rabbits
Half grown
Dashing across the fields
Then lost to eyes
That want to see

Peace so precious
Crows flew over
Without calling

Too beautiful a day
for hurrying

It would be over

Soon enough

Every five barred gate

Along his path

An invitation

To explore

Another world

Of adventure

Where he would slowly change

His role

Was not

to find

The sad injuries

And patch them

But simply

To observe

Refugee butterflies

And birds

Dance together

From thicket to thicket

Robin atop a tree

Quiet everywhere

Except for the throb

Of a near distant

Blind road

A day to walk

In parallel

To yourself

In order to gorge

Each self

On the beauty

That surrounds

And celebrate

Your unexpected

Part

A slim encounter

when asked
what would you like?
what is the need
that would bring the change?

He answered
A slim encounter
in the sun

a place
where
his body
could cry
its tears

all his anger
and
frustration
melted
into the sunlight

Where he could shine
just briefly
and his soul
could worship

all the beauty
of nature
glowing

in the fresh waters
of her peace

On the edge

what future winds
what past storms
were
the author
of his dreams

when you are there
on the tops
and the mists roll in
you don't know
where you are

even those places
you have known so long
look strange

shapes
loom
and leap
to confront you

fill each sinew
with fear
until it overflows

to be

slow

patient

unexpectent

but you have to be there

and when nature gives to you

then

you really are alive

It doesn't have to be

grand or dramatic

like a bird of prey

more likely small and exquisite

like the light

on a starling's chest

or beetle's wing

but it always does give

if you are there

The slight light rain

had ceased

On the cliff edge

A herring gull

shone bright

In the morning light

Perfect in grey and white

Challenging yellow beak

finished with a red spot warning

Below

the water was broken

by rocks

as it found its way shoreward

On its surface

The light sparkled

To the horizon

The Bird cast off

Into an enviable freedom

Melting into the light

How he longed

to do the same

and disappear

From the madness of the day

Reprise

He closed his eyes
To listen again
To the dawning Voice
of the black bird
and relive
those times
when he had felt
that senses were raw
in their sharing
and moved
with the inevitability
of a sea heading shorewards

linked
joyfully
with everything
that conjured his world

captured and distilled
the sweetness
to be supped
again

must be
with gentle moments
where
nature has relinquished
and given herself up to him

how rich
to be able
to recognise
those times

bees gathering
from
early morning flowers
that are reluctant
to open
to their purpose

tiny fox club
just six inches long
probing and
exploring
anew
a virgin world

Being Rich

how rich
some lives

Studland Shore

In a fire
Brightening circle

The sun
Spread the sea
From Horizon
To shore

a swimmer
Cut The chill of the waters

A crow
applauded
Head bobbing
its delight

warmth
ate softly through his being
fusing him
to every positive potential
of life

Washed clean

He lay
In that cool freshness
Of a night
Washed clean
By a fearsome rain
Which now
vainly
Tried

A reprise

He understood
Why he had so delighted
In the full refreshing sweetness
Of its flowing
So natural
So rare

Despite the lateness of the hour
The blind
Oblivion of sleep
That brings
A darkness of forgetfulness
Casting experience
Into careless unconsciousness
Eclipsing the moments
And bleaching them
From the mind

It was the very last
Feeling he required

To be awash
With nature's abundance
Was enough

Its memory
Came Rich
And truly sweet

Nature's Cathedrals

the light
embraced him
The evenings
were lengthening
so fast
running pell mell
from
the still point
of gloom

he walked
in a forest
Lost
Lost
In
the ghostly mystical hymn
Of gathering crows

Their voices
Absorbed and projected
in muted ricochet
from each
wonderfully drafted
wooden shaft

Mesmerized
Lost deep in their magic
Not needing
To understand

Not moving
But moved
he became marooned
in an intensity
of the lack of such things

Ageless notes
Reflections in the wind
Sounding through the years
Searching in unseen colours
Resisting answers
Yet ever asking 'why?'
Perhaps 'how?'
Never
'when?'

Rooftop Society

A Pigeon
Pink breast
Proudly
Gently
Puffed up and out
Confidently
Towards
The east
And the magic
Of the sun
Head slowly

Nature's Child

Occasionally
Tilted
To a new perspective

Just feet away
atop a covered chimney
Radiating white
To the rooftops
and the sky
Graded
To an excellent greyness
Not dull
But shining
Pink of leg
And yellow of Bill
A Herring Gull
Stands confident
Certain of the world
He surveys

Less sure
The pigeon
Quits the scene
Suddenly
Urgently

Enlivened
only in those moments
when Nature's children
Temporarily revealed themselves
And gave him their hand

he counted himself blessed
that Just occasionally
he had found
one of those
in a human form

From the earliest
times it was Nature
herself which held
the child under
her spell

A Secret Place

His secret place
Required
Passing through
The dapple light
Of woodland
Entering a darking Forest
Climbing a hillside
In a glaring dazzling daylight
Sliding down
Mountainside
releasing
his body
from all control

Then glimpsed
sparkling
Water
A stream
A pool
A sunburned rock
Naked
Like a Sacrifice

Naked toes

No sun today
he walked
amongst
the dunes
to save him
from the new wind
Under clouded skies

following
a well trod path
he was hers again
as ever should be
it was a good feeling to know

he could hear fresh voices
Of a thwarted spring

signs of life
hidden in the almost silence

intermittent moss
and sand
under his naked feet
between his naked toes

The Gift

watch the waters flow
and feel the freshness

a gift
in the sunshine
and
the shadows

Small Things

The purpose of his life
Had been
To understand
His smallness
On the face
Of the universe

a shaft of sunlight
parting the cold trees
to warm
a tiny once-drowned-body
into leg-kicking-life

a bird of prey on the wing
commanding
absolute attention
with a soul filled cry

Proud

my dog
chases strangers
from our territory
with his voice.

His tail
stands straight and Strong
like I've never seen
Life is so rich
and I fancy
I see
a vein
standing proud from his side
in the light which falls
from the kitchen window

Proud vein
White in the silver
of his Coat

Tendrils

His outward journey
Had been high and clear
Where free winds
Refreshed
Each moment
And blew away
The troubles cast

The return
The lower path
Less trod
where the spirit danced

From above and side
Nature sent tendrils
To snag and snare
To slow his gaze
So that he could see
The butterflies terpsicor

Around and through
The mysterious ferns
Woven by roots and branches
Of time sculpted trees
And thickets

Nettles snapped
at his naked muscles

A feather fell
From an open sky
Announcing its magic
Onto the ground

Very soon
He found another
To wonder
At its physics
Its geometry
Its engineering
Its ingenuity

when he touched
Life's softness
every part
of him
grew full
in that caress

and in its pleasure
shared

there was nothing more
nothing less

his nostrils
were filled
with
the soft
sweet smell

of
sun scorched
African earth
after the life giving rains

now
he could
rest content
in the pleasure
of that moment

so rare
so fleeting

The warmth
that brings him
back
chases away
his cold sleep

Sympathetic Planet

the constant rain
gentling its way
into the thirsty ground
soothing the greenness
back into the life

A shield bug landed
confident on his fingers
explored
and refused to leave
as if it had found
a sympathetic planet

Victory

Plumped up
and certain

Subtle shade
of mauve
pink
gorgeous grey
silhouetted
and
softly radiant
against
an embattled sky

Gaia

he walked
because he must

he remembered
how this ritual
had brought him
to her
long ago

All along the way
He called her name
Silently onto
the wind
That churns
waves and shore
repeating its chill
the one which lived
inside of him

On a sharp winter's day
When his every stride
Threatened
to
Shatter
the fragile ground
Beneath his step
Or
send his footfall skidding

The sun
could not
find its way
To warm him

Love fell
like snow
To turn
all around
to
a wonderland

And
The delicate things
it covered
achieved
their birthright
In their vulnerability

Sun walker

haunted by
a slow stalker

Sunbright sharp
a gull defeats
the frozen ground
with its flight

a dozen crows
on winter wood
stand sentry
over the stillness
hard against
the clear blue
of the day

Playing the wind

high above the shore
tossed crows
played the wind
How much he envied them

when they were done
a dozen crows
came to rest
on winter wood

Today

On the beach

Behold
The simple joy
Of dog
Racing
Chasing the tide
Free
From all
That is human

Solitary jackdaw
Turns seaweed
And announces
Herself
To a world

Her voice
falling deaf
Upon
Dead ears

And the Bird
Steps confidently
Along the breakwater
Now joined by another
Who had heard
her invitation to live

Old Dogs

When he looked into the face
of an old dog
who had been loved
it was a thing
he must love too

so it was
with anyone
who did not resist
their own history

Apricity

Someone
A stranger
sent me
a precious gift
a word
for the aftermath
of the lingering
and precious
warmth
of the sun
But
I lost it
I lost the word
but

I pray
I may
never
lose the feeling

I want
to die
in its embrace

Linked

joyfully
with everything
that conjured his world

He closed his eyes
To listen again
To the dawning Voice
of the black bird

To relive
those times
when he had felt
senses were raw
and moved
with the inevitability
of a sea heading shorewards

Egdon Heath

Giant sky

Heath
and Heather
Stretch forever

Skylarks sing
soar
and
Call a new lover
To a fragile nest

Mud puddle
dried by
Unpredicted warmth

Cracked and scored
An ancient map
For a life

Naked

The trees reveal
Their strength

Their allure
In flowing sculptures

Original
un matchable
They defy any human hand
To Frame and counterfeit their beauty

and please human eyes
to lead a heart
In infathomable ways

Lovely!

caterpillars
with point at each end
Just to fool me
And a reggae man
embracing the sunshine

Connecting

In the company of a dog

he had a touchstone

for all nature

An entree to the magic

it could hold

In him

Nature tripped

a sensing

of desire

not just his own

but hers too

running deeper

more open

not fired

by temporary longing

rather

something

he could savour

slowly

in every moment she dwelt

in his thoughts

sweet

and special

outside

of time

life took on

a relaxed urgency

to tell

all

of the little

he

had come

to understand

Virginia

as she waded

leadened legged

from skirts weighed down

with stones

each one so Care fully chosen

did she

note the leaves

signalling an urgent semaphor

by the side of the darkened waters

Did its chill

waken her

to the dancing grasses

the sparkling of the buttercups

amongst the green

Did she notice

the soft breeze

charm the light

on the broken surface

into her own ophelia reflection

did she hear

the Sweet exchanges

of the hopeful songsters

before her ears

were dulled

with the deep muffled roaring

of the waters flow

I would wager

it was so

Winter slumber

Dormant

she lay in the landscape

waiting

to be found

in any moment

The Gift

When a Robin

Is generous enough

To sit on a branch

And sing

Then

I should stand

And listen

Cycles

Feel the changes

See the why

And appreciate

Whatever colour

It might be

Dark or light

It was his own

Finally

Seeking alone

Feeling only the breeze

Watching the Cold waves

Kiss and embrace the shore

Disconnection

Humanity's unthinking conventions
were a brutal broom
Dissing the Planet
brushing away life
as it tried to establish
a fragile hold

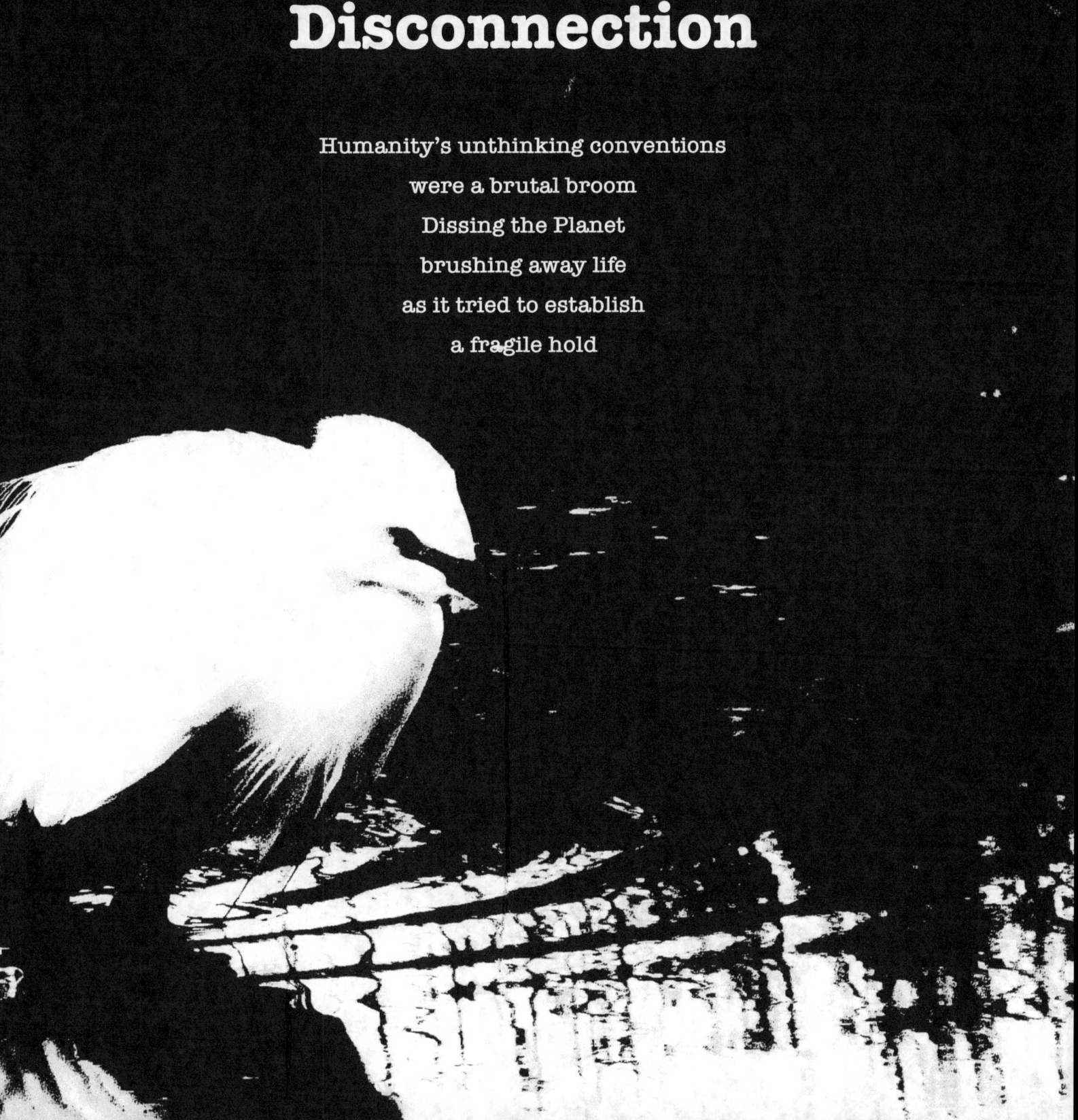

Cage Bird Song

The thwarted yearning of a heart
tears this world apart
A planet set on fire
by needless pointless desires
but Love for the smallest of things
Will make the world sing

The voice of a dog
Cast in the night
of a foreign land
told of prisoners
not lovers
Where normality
Is a host of cruelty
Looked upon
With indifferent eyes
And narrow minds

So sad for a life
she had not had.
No chance for bright tomorrow
locked in the sorrow
inside a cage
in a darkened room
breathing in an air of gloom

Lost from the skies
Uttering unheeded cries
Of hope for the sun

Hope for the one
Who will open the door
And let her soar

Free at last
Briefly
Enough time
To lose the past
And start to live
But who will give
This chance

It's a bird in the cage
That sets
All heaven in a rage
The sadness in their song
Tells of a wrong
Hearts full of sorrow
Will not bring
A good tomorrow

City Limits

Outside
The concrete fortress
Where the water
Washes away
The treeless
Rootless Fertility

To clog
The sudden fullness
Of a long Robbed
Brook and river
Reddened momentarily
Deep with hopeless
clogging
Choking
Flow
Bursting banks
With chemical poisons

The unbounded limits of the city
Radiate
Permeating the planet
with voices of greed
Trading parts
cut from imprisoned lives

Lost between two worlds
Nature's gifts
Squandered
on boardroom desks
and Stockmarket floors

Touching the face of god

To behold the face of god
He just had to look into nature

sadly what he saw there
was that their god
was being
defaced

How

How brief
the taste
Of what is sweet

The voice
of a bird
The fluttering purpose
Of a butterfly

How wasteful
How lingering
And unrelenting
The mundanity
Of human being

The Cry

his body ached
For the life affirming cry of the seagull

so easy
so natural
so far
from the voices
inside his head

Dodo bones

Safe behind the glass
Cased
obscured
From view
The murder
Of a branch
On the tree of life

The tortured pain
Of when
Flesh covered
A saddened heart
beat
inside

Autohuman

Soaked by
Uncertain
Unseasonable
Excessive rain
Falling from skies
Darkened and warmed
from Biochemical towers
Belching and retching
Mankind's
Foulness
Born from its excess
Destroying the earth

And he
was one of them
Inevitably so
Life confined by
mindless mauling mores

No independent
Thought
ever entering
Their birthTodeath
Programming

The sole marker of their sojourn
Scorched
Upon nature's demise

No more
Than automatic
Cogs in the machine

Bulldozing
Beauty
Under
inexorable
Progress

Disturbance in the night

Inseparable irrepairable pain
sits in the heart of life
Progeny of cold cruel witted complacency
With self-interested indifference
its sister

Fearful
Wandering
In the forest
Of the night

At each footfall
Spooked by ghosts
Of my own lifetime

The softness of the morning light
Reveals
The gentle trees
And beauty
Of the ground beneath his feet

Dream sellers

peddling
the king's
new clothes

happy to tell
naked lies

They're gonna
die alone
but they act
like
they don't know it

would they care
when they stand there
With nothing alive
inside

Ghost of A thing

Small
Almost inconsequential
The skeleton
Of the ghost
Of A thing
Scampered
Across his path

Recent and ancient
The ghost –of-the– thing
sat close inside
Close to his heart

Slowed each forward step
Wanting him to recognise
The part
It once played
To shape his life

Homeless

Darkroom
In a dark city
Where the dead
Fight their wars
And ghosts
Steal their light

From the dawn
Of burning fire

He couldn't go home
There was no place to go
Home
Was no longer anywhere

Only
Abandoned buildings
Where the seeds
Find a place to grow

And that makes him smile

Alarum

Blackbird's alarum
At the robbing
Of nature's light
Portent of a cold cold winter

Damp and chill
Swim around each naked part
Burying mellow melancholy
In each heart

A natural friend
A spore on the wind of change
Worrying the water

Dark car shadows
In cold streetlamplight

There was wonder
In the sounds
Of the night forest
It held magic
That few could feel
Or hear
Only primitive superstitious fears

The sort
That had
Driven a rift
between man and nature

unwilling
To accept
Their death as necessary
A part of the whole

Fighting a disease
Suffering
Locked within
A family body

Eventually
cutting down A tree
To make a box
In which a body
Will not rot

Gilded Cage

there are those
who say
they love birds
so they cage them
that they may be ready
to be ever present objects
for their whimsical
fleeting attention
until they die

within the cage
eyes grow dull
hearts cease to soar
feathers drop
or are ripped
from dis-heartened breasts

then the pacing begins
the rocking starts
and the madness
is hard to resist

Lament of a BSE Cow

Meat made me mad
Did it do
The same to you?

We need better kids for our world

Songs of the trees
whispering and shouting
their love of life
Dancing in their own rhythms

Earthbound

a dozen crows
on winter wood
night time owned
gathered to roost

Looking out
at a life
sketched in the lights
of distant towns

as he watched
the restive body of the hillside

moved in its grass and trees

darkened and misted
images shone
less brightly
spitefully
picking the pieces
from between the teeth
of wonder

soft whispering
came close
so easy
so natural
Like the surface of the sea
so far
from the voices
inside his head

His earthbound body ached
For each life affirming crowscry

Moth

Frightened
for the moth
that dances towards the light
knowing that soon
One will ride it down

A light you need
To carry you on
Wherever it will
No matter what ?

No hiding Place

Where He walked

There was

No Soul to be seen

The Cusp

Or found

Within him

At the cusp of the shore

It had been robbed

The seaweed tail

Or surrendered

Waved

By every wrong he had done

In the ceaseless serpent rhythm

mainly

eventually

Solitary jackdaw

To himself

Turns the weed

And announces

Rain had become so common

Herself

It Drenched him

To her world

To his skin

There was nowhere for cover

Her voice

No hiding place

falling deaf

Upon

Dead ears

And the Bird

Steps confidently

Along the breakwater

To be joined by another

Who had heard

her invitation to live

Zoo

Where does the zoo begin
Where can the heartache end
People all caged inside
And nowhere left to hide

Minds all cramped and hurt

Melting in the sun
With nowhere to run
People in their face
All they can do is pace

Up and down
Side to side
With nowhere to hide

Balancing

Watching the water's return
to level and balance
under the influence
of stars
and moon

He grew confident
in believing
that

under nature's influence
nothing is malevolent

but
He was certain
his kind would judge it so

Colours of life

Everything she was
Had held the colours of life

With a sorrow
As black as raven's
Robbed and broken feather
She walked the island paths

Tattoos of her heart
Tossed with the winds
Fleetingly highlighted
Between the shadows
Cast by the Leaves

on the tops
and the mists rolled in
even those places
She had known so long
looked strange

shapes loomed
and leapt
to confront her
filling each sinew
with fear

it overflowed
As Earth's midnight passed

Knowing there was Little hope
For the new born

See what they want to see
And disregard the rest

Butterfly wings

Butterfly wings
which do no harm
are destroyed by the
light
of the candle they seek.
How long then we....

Forlorn Hope

Super razor sharp surreal light
Cracking the Black

A hint of the ancient promise
buried deep

That the earth can undo
The Blighting World of Men

A calling card
That few
Will see

Left for men
Who will

The Fly

Why does
the buzzing of a fly
desperate to free itself
from our presence
disturb us so
Unsettle our peace
distract our mind

Does it make us recognise
our own confinement
in this human world
?

Behind Closed Doors

He had always wanted more

As they wrestled
with the way the people lived
ugly amongst the debris
they have scattered

Blue metal skin
Stifled cries
Villains' souls
Pressed into their bodies

Rusty treasures
Condemned the trap
If it had been good
There was no fanciful reward
Spiritual or material
For wasting the world

The idea
That the infinite was in everything
Was their greatest
deliberate misunderstanding
All for the sake of their comfort

On the bank by moonlight
Charmed by the sound
Of the night
Was it shifting
Releasing him
For what lay within

Mistaken eyes
Searching for an impulse
Thralled to serendipity
Unbuckled
From the longing to be
Empty

In bright fluorescence
bent and shaped
The words told
Everything that
lives is holy

It glared
Blinding his eyes

Where was the change in vision
He sought
No place
For the sensitive soul
With no way home

Pimping for the man
Bandits known in life and film
Easy to recognise
And no heroes to be admired

Beirut emptying its rubbish into the
Ocean
Claiming to reclaim the land
Which was never there
or would be

Tears frozen into canvas

Splashed to reflect
destruction's distribution

Saga of the spreading
Of the planet's dissolution
A long-long journey
Layered
Beautiful and broken

Soles that crush
The souls of life
Eviscerating the solemn bond
obliterating the rainbow from the sky

Philistine rulers
Prosperous peasantry
Charred and broken

Seasons in hell
Floating in space
Outcast
Of its own soul

Beyond recovery
In the death of vision
Sacrificed on the alter of forbidden
fires

The killer was already on the road
systematic derangement
of the sense
Of reason
For being there

Acid crooning
sinister threatening
Winding
around all that was worth living for
Strangling the light within

A lost and abandoned eternity
will hold us the guilty
And curse us for it

We were never aware of the
other possibilities

Naked existence
Within
And without
Wasting and withering

Tormented

Heaven's prisoner
Surveying the end
Of every lovely thing

Could you ever imagine
That the completed contract
Would come to this
Who would've thought

This would be the eventual outcome
Of human love's purpose
Who could see that it would
be the finish of everything

Destination—Termination

Light Pollution

every day held in it
the possibility of rebirth
from the darkness
of the night

But a ceaseless
Light in that night
was Cheating the birds
Of their sleep

demanding they sacrifice
their precious voice
to a constant day

Rich Madness

Exploiting their madness
Counting their wealth
Inside
The
Moon
Light
Reflected
on
Each
Dark
Crevice

Where they seek
To hide
Their darkness
In the darkness
From the darkness

Prison guards

The answer
I was only doing my job
Held no purchase
As he stared down that barrel of a gun

All those who felt they were saved for
heaven
Who had Gathered
Their riches on earth
And were bound for Glory
Faithful servants
Of their master
Gathered together
And boarded their
Luxury ships

Each set off from the planet
They had laid to waste

As they travelled
Hulls began to rust

And their cargo was jettisoned
Into the vast frozen darkness

On earth those who remained
The meek
Who were
Left behind
Congratulated each other
On a job well done

Vivisection

T'was the night before Christmas
All through the house
Not a creature was stirring,
not even a mouse

They were all locked up in laboratories

Love's Elegy

Running away
Unhappy prey
Of winter weather

Against the joy of the sun
A child separated from its mother

In the tearing
Of an image
Sabat
Love's elegy for the earth

Winter has caught me
Wanting to be free
From the cruelty
Perpetuated day on day
Hour on hour
On those with whom
We share the earth

Each one a slave
Awash in the ugliness
But declaring
Whatever they suffered
That was okay
As long as
We treated them well

And the bible
Says it's so

Consequences

Soon the people were
Charging the gates of hell

"Welcome guys
Come right on in!"

There they would cry
" less travail
Less travail"
A constant wail

Day and night
" Pity our plight"
They cried
And were gleefully denied

To the keeper's ears
t'was a delight
A charm
At balm
To soothe
And bring such calm
As he had never had
To know they were so sad
So so sad

He cast an inward eye
Across the memory
Of the desolation

Each one had wrought
In pursuit
For things they bought
Without a second thought
Of the cost
Or what was lost

Ever Constant War

Even before the ever constant war
With its untraceable beginning

It seems there was no time
that Animal life
Was not Marked for extermination

Few were willing to stand
Against the slaughter

Old age has no blessing
In the question
Why didn't we do
Something?

Surrendering
the polar bear seas
To the treachery of black oil

Taking to the Streets

Autumn winds
Had blown Summer into a memory

The sky was bright
The air bearably Sharp

She did not want
To leave the house
Although it was cold
And lonely inside

The Surrey Hills
Were respectable
He was respectable
That was the story
That was why they lived there

What he did was
Far from worthy
Of any respect

He brokered
destruction
On the earth

You can only talk
With actions
And she had taken hers

Frozen stone steps
Were no colder
Than his heart

The empty space
Where it could have been
Grew wider
Year on year

He would call to her
Every day
But in the place
She lay
She would never hear

How many
Long gone lonely heartbeats
Had the world measured
What was the cost
In pain and goods?

Appetites

Regaled
By a strange hunger
That is overfull
Yet demands more
And more
In search of sweetness
To fill
An unrelenting
Unfulfilled
Happytimeappetite

Changes

His scream was silent
No voice
Could be heard
or was needed

To try
Would be pointless

Observed from now
Life was a reservoir
Of wasted moments

He had squandered
The choice in each one

Links to nature
Grew stronger

Not just to things that moved
but things that grew
From the soil
Whatever it would be

Unfulfilled

A Robin Song
Truncated
Stopped short
For all time

And A Car rolls on
Leaving silence

A Gibbon's call
Missing from the sunrise

Instead a soaring sawing

So much silent pain
Is Overwhelming

He thinks of a long gone lover
Rails at a rotten referee
Anything to fill that silence

Silence that lets him know
Makes him think
Life is precious
When you're in it

You cannot divide the death
Each murder is as one

Evanescent 2

A tern
Caught within the light
Of the new moon
Playing sweetly
Gentle on the sea

To be a child
In the church
Of the wild
Swimming there
Rain washing skin

Iridescent blue
Break upon break
Shining sliver sleeper
Slithers
In the mirror of memories

Regrets
Sorrows
Sadness
and Anger
Mingling in the elusive lie
Sweet as chocolate
Bitter as wormwood

To heal the heart
Expel the intangible hurt
Promising hope
To desperate eyes
Gazing full-mooned
Upon an orphaned forever

Laying up
An undesirable store
Against the coldest
Of winters

Evanescent 3

Evermore crude
and superficial
Words
That own the past

Kicking hard at the ground
In anger
Reaching blind
at the night

Light
shining high above
In the world
never to be captured

Sacrificed
to
unreasonable
unfulfillable
demands

Transcendent
Eclipsing the sky
Blown away
Into the face of God

Full of fear
Victim of greed
In its timelocked mind

Physical never spiritual
Dying of a broken heart

Longing for the relief of an explosion
From inside
Intimate ruinous singularity
A way of looking ample
Where the trees can dance no more

Locked into space
Unable to celebrate in love
Galvanised instead
in the love of war

Beautiful peace
of a thrusting canine face
Feeling everything truly
As it should be

Safe in bed
unwilling to share
seeking a peppermint tranquillity
Alone into a wonder full Ness

and no one to see

Timeless Riches

when he thought about being rich
money never entered his mind

only nature
and its touch
as it
inveigled itself
into his very being
saturated
his soul
and made the life
he shared
as one with the earth
on which his
feet fell so heavily

his aspiration
was all for Her
that She should remain
unassailed
unspoiled
Unplundered

Psychopathology

Nature's gifts
Squandered
On Boardroom Desks
And
Stockmarket Floors

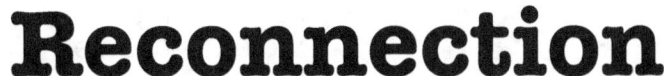

Reconnection

(Threads of Hope)

(With Thanks for Greta)

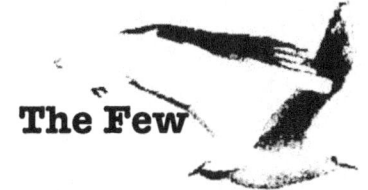

The Few

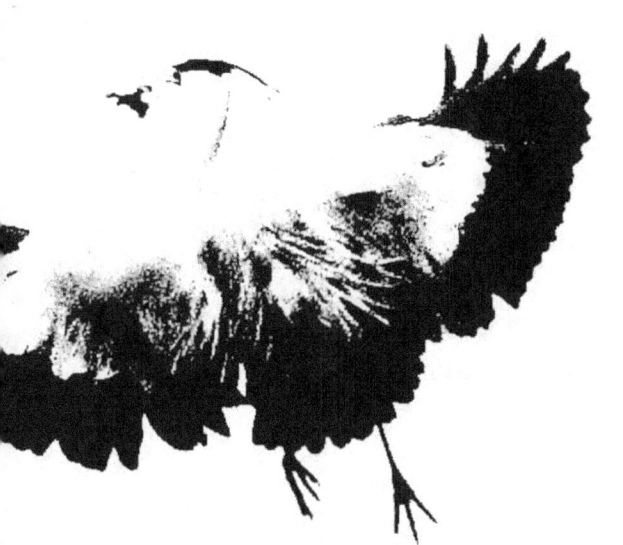

The threat
Seen in the sky
By a keen
Portentous eye

The alarm
Raised
By one
Then another

Suddenly aware
The crows take to the wing
To mob
And drive away
The danger

Cracking the Black

a shaft of sunlight

parting the cold darkness

with a soul filled cry

A hint of the ancient promise

buried deep

That the Earth can undo

The Blighting World of Men

Despite the lateness of the hour

To be awash

With nature's abundance

Its memory

Comes Rich

Its purpose

To understand

Our smallness

On the face

Of the universe

Longing to see

The world wild again

Like a child again

To be beguiled again

Bewitched by Nature

Enthralled

to all that surrounds us

Bothered and bewildered

By what

And how

we had become

Fearing

what was wild

Embracing only

The safe and sterile

So ugly inside and out

Petrified of the freedom

We deny

To the rest of life

Now seeking to plant

A spring

That is

No longer

Silent

Healing Company

The irresistible company of dogs
Holds an ever-present promise

No matter how far back
In time it may lay
The wilderness is part
Of the soul of a dog

To discover
The longing for that place
Is vital for those
who want to survive

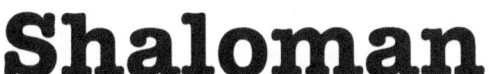

Shaloman

The question was

why had the humans destroyed

the once blue planet?

He knew the reason

Many

very many

believed

he was the reason

And history

had it had a chance

to be written

would have agreed

No one knew
when Shaloman appeared amongst them

Legend said
it was on the African plains
long ago

His dress was strange
He had wrapped himself against the world
and all it held
Holding only the cold inside

Totally without conscience
or empathy
His only charm used
to seduce to his purpose
Life was for the taking
was his only certainty

Everyone who looked on his face
saw what he wanted them to see

When he talked
they heard only
what they had wanted to hear

In those moments
their vision
was limited for ever
blinkers on their eyes

the grooming begun

He was there
to show them
how to dominate
not share

He sent them
one and all
happy shameless hypocrites
shambling through the planet
with no understanding
of what was true
only what is new

In the name of a knowledge
falsely conceived
with their cataract gaze
they vivisected earth's life

Ever full
they fed their greed
and refused to accept
they too
were to be shaped by the world
in which they lived

Complacent
they refused
to concede consequences

to all they had done

happy to live in contradictions

every day

comfortably ensconced

within the ideal

that ignorance was truly blissful

Imperial peddlars

they paid the piper

and called the tune

created their own gods

gave them voices in scriptures and stories

a cynical profanation

what should have been sacred

was plundered from the earth

Bullying and intimidating

The greedy grew powerful

exploiting the meek and peaceful

who lived close to Nature still

Throughout the ages

The stars bore witness

to what they had done

Shaloman conducted their dance

spinning on the wheel of time

circling the truth

no-one daring to step out of line

In the name of profit

they rode into battle

ruthless towards

whatever stood in their way

"Grow grow grow the profits fiercely up

the graph"

the anthem they sang

until there was nothing left to be had

Life's oasis lay naked

Marooned in a hostile Space

they proved themselves

the most hostile agents

of the earth's destruction

Charred skeletons of the trees

bore the strange fruit of a cruelty

wrought by blind hatred

and self loathing

The faded grandiose streets of the City

pockmarked

with fiendish murder sites

piled high with the bodies

of their fellows

animal and human

held promise of gold

robbed from far off places

Far off beaches
lay scattered with the debris
of their indifference

A fetid smell began
in waste dumped there
and carried on the winds
to their cocaine damaged noses

They created laws
for the powerful
by the powerful
Each law a heinous crime
to keep safe the booty
stolen from the earth
With plenty
to mindlessly
Follow their bidding

Second coming believers
climate change deniers
wildlife destroyers
ocean polluters
fitted so well into Shaloman's plan

giving away the best of themselves
Not hearing the trumpeted prophecies
that there was to be no resurrection
Dead veins would not flow again
Dead ears would never hear
an honest truth

Predacious humanity
preying on the planet
thinking to bring their salvation
certain
when they had laid waste the earth
Their Christ would return

Final Cloud

Finally

The cloud was coming

Slowly

Inexorably

From the west

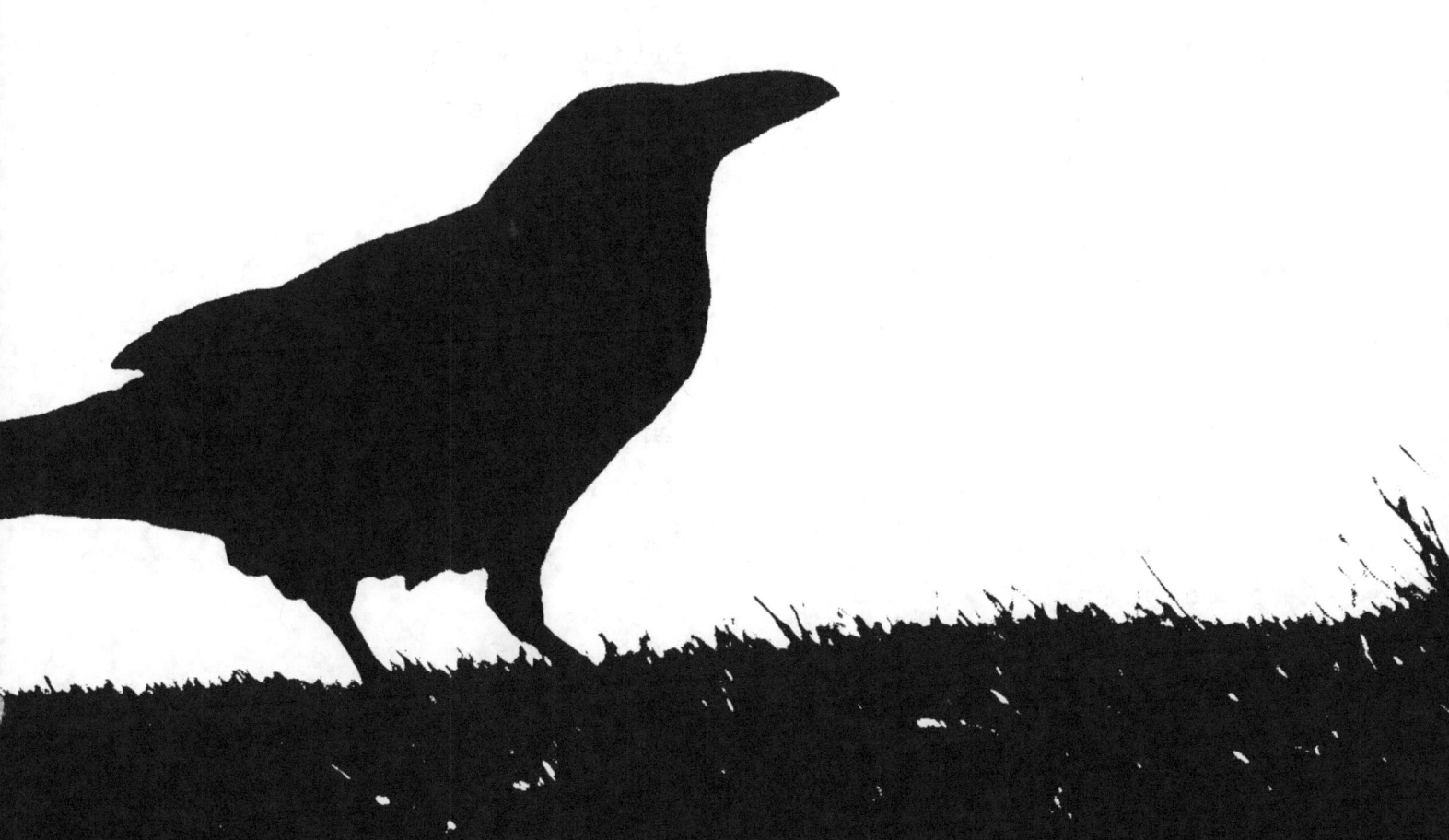

The people
Gathered
On the cliff
To see their fate
Approaching

Their crimes
Against the world
Howled loud
in the following wind

They Watched
As seabirds
Fell stone like
From
Blackened air
Engulfed
in its choking mass

The people cried out
Why?
How?
Who?

It wasn't me
It wasn't us!

Deep from within
that desperate denial
a young girl's voice
Full of tears

For things
She Loved
Called out
Of course it was!

The people turned
to shout her down
Foolish Child!

Angry
as her words
echoed deep
inside Each one
To tell them
That her voice was true

Each one had done the deal
Had sold the world
For a mess of potage

Complacent
Comfortable
In conforming
To consuming
Trinkets
That they had been
Told to buy

No accounting
After the True
Cost

For years
Flowers had ceased to bloom

Still the people took
And took
Faster
To comfort them
Against what was missing

They had forgotten
Chosen not
To remember
When the wind
Blew pure

Now it carried
Their inevitable death

In their homes
Or in landfill sites
The trinkets rotted

The people should have known
When the prophets
Left
Tired of their ways
Bereft of all hope

They had watched them go
And not understood

The People had mourned
The prophet's passing
As was proper
As they should
As was required

Then it had been
business as usual
Words rang
From Devices
Tracked inside their heads

And the words said
Buy this product!
Own it
And it will set you free

You don't have
To worry
Your pretty heads
Anymore

Don't seek a meaning
It is not important

The voice of the child
Which so many had Heard
Continued to cry
No!

The command came back
Don't listen to her words

If you are not
A material junkie
You are nothing
And you deserve to die

On the hill
Above the crowd
The old man walked
A Fool on the hill
He did not
understand these people

Who were they?
What was their reason

Long ago
He had
Set himself apart
Separated
Holy in a bubble
Of his own time

He had tried
To send
Messages
Out from within this sphere

They clapped

And whistled
And cheered
Believing that was enough

They did nothing
Letting Time speed by
Living in a soap opera
Safe and sound

The Fool's words
Became foolish to them

In a mist of confusion
They blamed him
For the what he had said
Words they did not want to hear
Or heed

What he tried to give them
They did not want
It did not glisten
It did not sparkle

He had given
All he had away
Enough is plenty
Is what he would say
And yours is not the way

He was looking to the sun
And they were in the darkness

Of the bargain bargain basement
Searching for something
That might just bling

The candle of his life
Burned slowly
Flickering
Within his eyes

Fed by the warmth it made
In his belly
It had made him
Whatever he was

A one-day hero
Was never
Going to be
Enough

What was required
Was living the everyday
Face to face
Challenging
The madness

The cough
had started slow
It stayed
It spread
A subtle contagion
More subtle

Than anything
they lived by

Left and right
It spread
A portent of what was to come

Pretending their innocence
Denying their murderous guilt
Looking to blame someone
Anyone else

Why?
Was the cry
Spluttering from each choking throat

Above them in the mist
They spied the man
Who had foretold this moment

Hands pointing
Voices screamed
There!
He's the one!

United in their hatred
Baying in one rhythm
Of familiar loathing
They ran upon the hill
Into the mist
Searching desperately

For one last lie
To absolve them
A Catholic confession
Relieving all responsibility

Instead of the fool
They found a tree
They tore at it
To expose a hollow shell

They burned the tree
And the tree burned them
Smoke rose into fetid air
Rising from their rotting bodies
And joined the incoming cloud

Overwhelmed
with sorrow

Not for what
They had done
Not for the birds
Falling from the air
Not for the grass
Dying beneath their tread

Only for themselves

They had believed
The false promise
That it would last for ever

However long
The countdown had been
This was the end of it

The Child gathered the tree's ashes

With her last strength
She cast them into the air
To be carried
In the dying dream
That they would float out
Far into
A benign universe

Where homo sapiens
Could not reach
To place their poisonous step

Lyrics

Do you tell

Do you tell your children what you do
When they want to tell you
The things they've heard
That can't be true

About the men they've learned to hate
Who have cast their future to a hopeless
fate

Surely it can't be the same one
Who kept them safe when they were young
The one whose always made things right
Reassuring the darkest fright

Now he sells life into constant night
A man with heart as cold as ice
Who'd sell his soul if the price is right

Do you tell your children what you do
When they want to tell you
The things they've heard
That can't be true

If you really want it
Then it will stop

The stories always been the same
Life Bought and sold
For greed and gain

What kind of mother
Could turn aside
And simply ignore
The coming tide

Watching bonds
As old as time
Be ripped apart
In heartless crime
Prisoners of hearts
As cold as ice
Making other's lives
Pay the price

Do you tell your children what you do
When they want to tell you
The things they've heard
That can't be true

If you really want it
then it will stop

Just wanting it won't make it right
If you want it we have to fight
If changing lives is the plan
Come on and show us you're a real man

It's not so hard
Start from here
Give up trading
In the market place of fear

Melt that heart
As cold as ice
Stop making the planet
Pay the price

Would you care
Would you dare
To tell your children what you do

WOT! NO MEAT?!

Performed by Captain Sensible & Rachel
Bore Released 1983 on Animus Records

What have we made of this world
Every way
Every turn
It's a battle
There a war going on
between man and the birds, beasts
and cattle.

The front line is there in your eyes.
Don't do all the things you'd despise
But, of course, you can change it

Who are we to demand all those lives
Why should creatures pay our price
the blinkers are there on our eyes
and yet we seem so nice

To the man who kills with no need
If he realised on what he feeds
He would change it

The businessmen hold all the cards
They think they're so healthy
Their ploy is to fatten the calves
Just to feed all the wealthy

You wonder why the hell there are
wars
When in truth all the answers are
yours
But, of course, you can change it

Chorus written by Sensible

I'm not so meat crazy
It's not so neat baby
Wot! No Meat?

Earth Mother

Now is the time
For us to come together
We need to change the weather
Every boy
Every girl
Must work for our world

Each woman
Each man
Needs to understand
the earth
Is our mother
Sister and Lover

She is the reason
We are alive

She must be the reason
That we live

What have we done
To our sweet mother

Beaten and stabbed her
Stripped her bare

And lying naked there

Tied her down

to Cut her hair

Burned her body

Tortured and killed her children
every day by the billion

We have become you and I
A cancer on her face
A human race
To destruction
To extinction

A population timebomb
Which Long ago exploded

Driven by a stampede
Fuelled by fear and greed
Sold as dreams
by men in mean suits

Profiteers who want it all
Just don't care
What is the price
Rob and kill with sneers

State backed pirates
Who won't count the cost
Of anything they do
They feed on me and you

Because the blinkers are there

on our eyes

And yet we seem so nice

About the author

Writer, poet, sculptor, Saatchi-shortlisted artist, award-winning photographer, lyricist and environmentalist, Geoff Francis' life-long concern for the planet powers his creative output and practical initiatives. He set up and ran the first paper recycling campaign in London for the nascent Friends of the Earth.

A long-time advocate for animals, he also set up and ran Animaline for Linda McCartney, Carla Lane and Rita Tushingham. Geoff has been vegan for 50 years. He also has a long-term involvement with Hillside Animal Sanctuary and is a trustee of Journey's End Animal Sanctuary in Florida.

Other vegan enterprises include Fruits of the Earth frozen vegan foods, Pacific Isle Cruelty Free Soaps, Animus Badges, Animus Records and Rosalie's Good Eats Cafe in Central London.

He co-founded No More Dodos, a charity using art and sport to raise awareness and inspire change and positive action for the Planet.

Other Titles by Geoff Francis

Poetry

A Breath Before Dying
ISBN 978-1-907729-30-0
SAILORS
ISBN 978-1-907729-25-6
LOST WANDERINGS
ISBN 978-1-907729-17-1
FOUND
ISBN 978-1-907729-23-2
unNATURAL HEART
ISBN 978-1-907729-19-5

Poetry and Photographs

LOVE LOOKS
ISBN 978-1-907729-06-5
I WANT TO SEE
ISBN 978-1-907729-07-2

Fiction

A Badger's Tale -Eric Ashby Edition
ISBN 978-1-907729-18-8
A Badger's Tale- Naturewatch Foundation Edition
ISBN 978-1-907729-37-9
Babylon Farm
with Paintings by Geoff Francis
ISBN 978-1-907729-17-1
Or is it?
with images by Paul Windridge
ISBN 978-1-907729-20-1
Spirit of the Game
ISBN 978-1-907729-08-9
Spirit of the Game Audio Book
ISBN 978-1-907729-24-9

Non-fiction

Stanley Matthews The Black Man with a White Face
ISBN 978-1-907729-02-7
Celebrity Vegetarian Cookbook with Janet Hunt
ISBN 1-85425-017-5